At a Glance™
Series

DVD and Lesson Book

DVD Blues Guitar

T0071567

By Merv Young

Video Performers: Doug Boduch, Tom Kolb, and Wolf Marshall

ISBN: 978-1-4234-4297-4

HAL•LEONARD®
CORPORATION

7777 W. BLUEMOUND RD. P.O. BOX 13819 MILWAUKEE, WI 53213

Visit Hal Leonard Online at
www.halleonard.com

Table of Contents

Introduction

The blues has been an inspiration to countless guitarists for many decades. An experienced blues player can squeeze a whole range of human emotions out of the guitar using only a handful of notes. This enduring appeal will ensure that the blues remains an essential element of every guitarist's bag of licks.

If you've only recently started playing the blues, or if you're in need of some fresh inspiration, then *DVD Blues Guitar*, from Hal Leonard's exciting At a Glance series, is just what you need. The emphasis here is on getting you playing right away, so you'll find a whole stack of riffs, licks, chord ideas, and turnarounds presented in a snappy and fun manner. The series also uses real songs by real artists to illustrate the techniques and concepts that you'll learn along the way. In *Blues Guitar*, you'll learn licks and riffs from B.B. King's "The Thrill Is Gone," Stevie Ray Vaughan's "Pride and Joy," Robert Johnson's "Sweet Home Chicago," Robben Ford's "Mama Talk to Your Daughter," and many more!

Additionally, each book in the At a Glance series comes with a
DVD containing video lessons that correspond to the printed
material. The DVD that accompanies this book contains four
video lessons, each approximately eight to ten minutes in length,
that correspond to the topics covered in *Blues Guitar*. In these
videos, ace instructors Doug Boduch, Wolf Marshall, and Tom
Kolb will show you in great detail everything from how to play
blues shuffles to seamlessly combining different scale ideas when
creating a blistering blues solo. As you progress through *Blues
Guitar*, try to play the examples first on your own, and then check
out the DVD to see if you played them correctly. As the saying
goes, "A picture is worth a thousand words," so be sure to use
this invaluable tool on your quest to becoming an accomplished
blues guitar player.

THE BLUES SCALE

The blues scale is very common in many different styles of music, from blues and rock to country and jazz. We're going to learn all about it and apply it to many different licks and riffs, so grab your pick and let's get started.

The Minor Pentatonic Scale

First off, let's talk about where the blues scale comes from; it's based on an even more common scale called the *minor pentatonic* scale. Even if you haven't heard of the term "minor pentatonic scale" before, you've definitely heard the scale used in literally millions of rock, blues, jazz, and country tunes, not to mention many other styles.

It's composed of the root, $\flat$3rd, 4th, 5th, and $\flat$7th degrees of the natural minor scale. The natural minor scale contains seven notes, whereas the minor pentatonic scale is a shortened version of this, containing only five notes—hence the "penta" of pentatonic, meaning "five." The notes that are removed from the minor scale to make it a five-note scale are the 2nd and the $\flat$6th.

A natural minor scale	A	B	C	D	E	F	G
	Root	2nd	$\flat$3rd	4th	5th	$\flat$6th	$\flat$7th

A minor pentatonic scale	A		C	D	E		G
	Root		$\flat$3rd	4th	5th		$\flat$7th

Here's the scale for you in the key of A minor. Check out the DVD to see the fret-hand fingering.

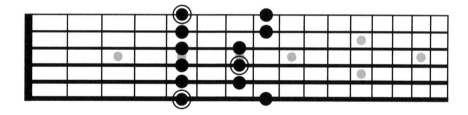

The Blues Scale

To turn our minor pentatonic scale into a blues scale, all you have to do is add one note: the $\flat$5th.

A blues scale	A	C	D	E$\flat$	E	G
	Root	$\flat$3rd	4th	$\flat$5th	5th	$\flat$7th

The $\flat$5th is also known as the "blue" note, so you know right away it's an important note in the scale. And it really does help to make things "bluesy." Here's the A blues scale for you. This also starts on fret 5.

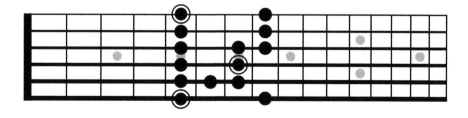

Both of these scale shapes are moveable shapes. This means that, if you want to play a G blues scale, you just take the A blues scale shape and move it down two frets so the whole pattern starts on fret 3. It's nice and easy to change keys on the guitar! If you want to play a B minor pentatonic scale, take your A minor pentatonic shape and move it up two frets so the whole pattern starts on fret 7.

Blues Scale Exercises

Let's get more acquainted with the blues scale by playing some exercises to help you get it under your fingers. The first one involves the lower octave of the scale and will be played on the low E, A, and D strings.

 This is in 3/4, which means we're counting 3 beats for each measure (or bar). Watch the DVD carefully to see what fingers are used to fret the notes in these exercises. Make it a point to try and avoid using the same finger to play consecutive notes that are on the same string. Playing with the same finger might seem easier at first, but using different fingers will enable you to develop speed and fluency.

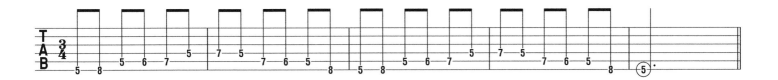

You'll see on the DVD that this exercise is played using *alternate picking*, or down-and-up picking. If you don't know how to do this and tend to pick everything in the same direction, then this is a great exercise with which to practice the alternate picking technique. Expect this to be a bit fiddly at first until you get used to it! When you do get the hang of it, your speed should really start to develop.

Speaking of speed and accuracy, be sure to practice these exercises with a metronome. If you don't have a metronome, then shame on you! Get out to the music store and buy one right now. It will prove to be one of the best investments you've ever made. Start slowly at first and make sure every note is played clearly and cleanly. Then start to increase the metronome speed each day by small increments.

 The next exercise contains exactly the same notes we just played but in the upper octave, which means we'll be playing predominantly on the G, B, and high E strings.

Before things get a little trickier, let's put these two exercises together into an A blues scale played across all six strings that covers two octaves.

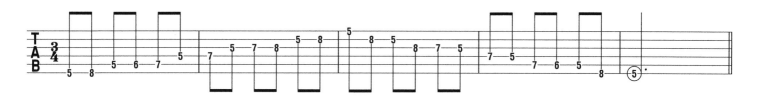

These exercises work great for warming up before practice or warming down afterward. Here's one more exercise using the A blues scale in a sequenced triplet rhythm. The pattern behind this sequence is as follows: play a note, then go up to the next note in the scale, and then come back down to the original note. This pattern is done starting on each note of the scale. And since these are triplets, you'll be playing three notes per beat. Be careful with the timing at the beginning here as the exercise starts on the "and" of beat 4. Check it out on the DVD.

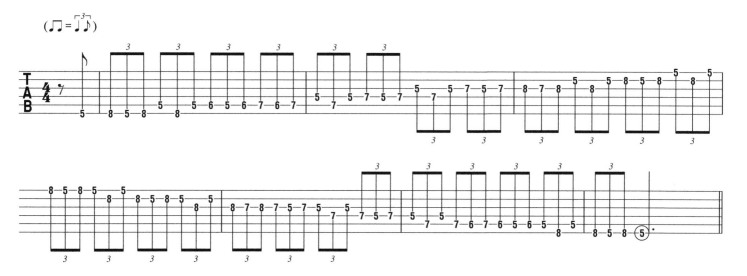

Here's another pattern that will move you across all six strings using non-stop eighth notes. Again, take it slowly at first and build up your speed with the metronome.

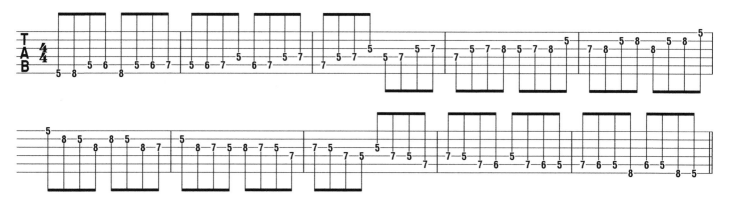

Blues Scale Licks

We've been playing the blues scale so far in the box 1 position. This is probably the most commonly used position on the fretboard to play both the blues scale, and the minor pentatonic scale. Let's check out some cool licks to play using the blues scale in this position.

Here's our first one. As with the triplet exercise you just played, this also starts on the "and" of beat 4.

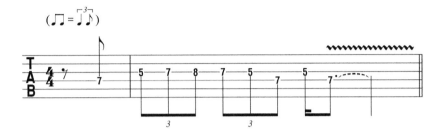

Notice the tasty vibrato used on the last note to give it a bluesy vibe. Take the time to master these tasteful techniques as they're critical to the emotion that is inherent within the blues.

Here's another blues lick that includes a string bend from the 4th up a half step to the flat 5th; that's our "blue" note—remember? This one also starts on the "and" of beat 4.

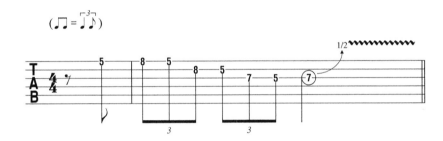

On the string bend, pull the string down toward the floor or push it toward the ceiling just enough to hit the right pitch. You can check your target pitch, the flat 5th, by just playing the fretted note on the eighth fret of string 3. You might also want to try singing the note on fret 8 as you bend up from fret 7. This will help to get your ears tuned in to what you're playing too.

When you're comfortable with the string bend, try adding a little vibrato to the bent note. Watch this carefully on the DVD to see how it's done. This is a great technique but can be tricky to make sound smooth and even, so persevere.

The next idea is a short exercise that takes string bending a stage further. This time you have to bend up a half step from fret 7 and then, without picking the string again, release the bend bringing it back to the original, unbent pitch. This should be a smooth and even up-and-down sound.

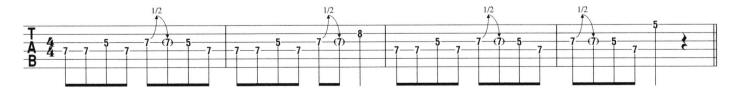

The symbol above the time signature (that you've seen a few times now) tells you to play this next lick with a shuffle or swing feel. This means to play the eighth notes unevenly in a shuffle rhythm. Check out the DVD to hear how this sounds. It's a very familiar sound that's best explained with a demonstration. This one starts on the "and" of beat 3.

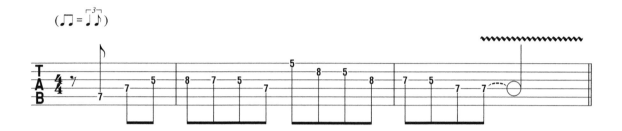

The DVD also includes this lick being played without the shuffle feel so you can hear the difference between shuffled eighths and straight eighths, which is what we call regular eighth notes that aren't shuffled. Keep yourself nice and relaxed as you're playing this lick through and make sure you can play it with both the swing feel and the straight feel. If you're still not sure about this feel, check out the examples at the start of the Blues Rhythm chapter.

It's worth remembering that all of these licks can be applied to other styles as well, such as rock, blues rock, country, bluegrass, jazz, and more. Try speeding them up or slowing them down, playing them with a clean sound, or with a whole bunch of distortion. You can also try changing some of the notes or rhythms.

Other Blues Box Positions

Now we're going to look at the other box positions on the fretboard where you can play the notes of the blues scale and the minor pentatonic scale that we looked at earlier. There are a total of five boxes that will enable you to play in the same key across pretty much the whole guitar neck. We've already studied the first box of the A blues scale, so we'll keep the rest in the same key.

Here's box number two; watch the DVD carefully for the fret-hand fingerings.

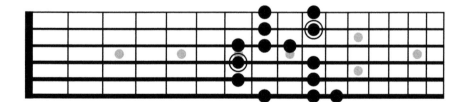

Remember, these are all the same notes as box 1 (A–C–D–E♭–E–G) but just in a different position on the fretboard.

Here's Box 3.

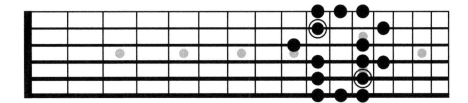

And on to Box 4.

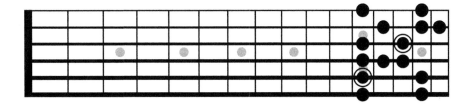

The Box 4 shape also works really well down in open position for this key. It's still the same shape as we had on fret 12, but those open strings sure make it great for a country blues twang or some Texas blues.

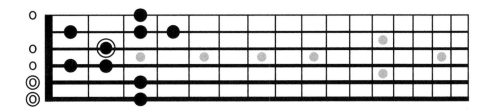

As we've now moved down the fretboard, we'll play the Box 5 shape at fret 3.

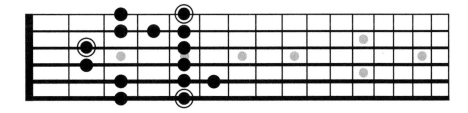

That's a whole stack of scales to learn, so take your time to get them under your fingers. Remember that these shapes are moveable. The root notes are circled on each box shape, so just move the shape up or down the fretboard until one of the circled notes is in the correct position for the new key.

11

You should try writing your own licks in all these box positions; the different patterns will inspire different phrases and sounds. You can also play most of these boxes up an octave (twelve frets higher) depending on how many frets your guitar has!

Riffs

 We've played a lot of scales, licks, and exercises so far. Now let's play some fun blues scale riffs as well. This one is kind of funky.

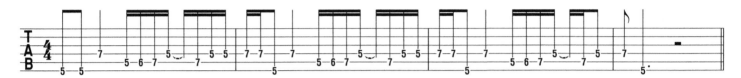

 This next one is a shuffled bluesy riff. The bends are only a quarter step, so you just need to bend a little bit to achieve the right sound. Use your pinky to play the bent note on fret 8, string 6. This will mean your index finger is ready to grab the low A on the sixth string, fifth fret.

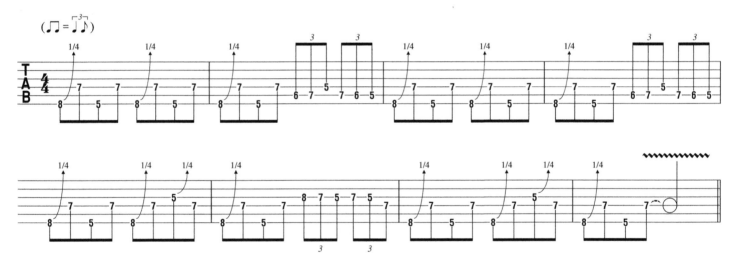

On the DVD, notice that, for the eighth notes in the riff, the notes on the sixth string are being played with a downstroke of the pick, and the notes on the fourth string are being played with an upstroke.

Next we have a pentatonic riff that features some double stops with some subtle bends in places. Get your first finger holding down the two notes at the same time and bend the strings down gently.

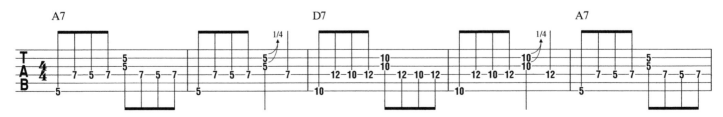

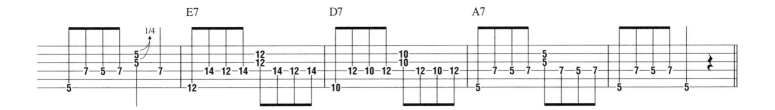

Practice playing these blues scale patterns, licks, riffs, and exercises in different keys as well. They're all moveable patterns, so all you have to do is shift your hand position to a different fret and you're in a new key.

To finish off let's check out how some of the blues greats use these scales.

First off we have the opening four bars of "Steppin' Out" as played by Eric Clapton with John Mayall's Bluesbreakers. There are subtle bends and big bends here, so follow it carefully. Try to get your speed up too—this one's fast!

"STEPPIN' OUT"
Eric Clapton

Words and Music by
James Bracken

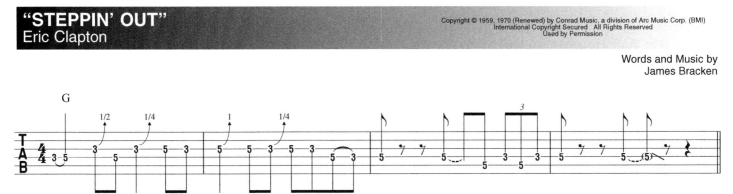

This next one is a great riff from "I Got My Eyes on You" by Buddy Guy. The dots above some of the notes indicate a staccato feel. This means these notes should be cut short. To do this, immediately release pressure in the fretting hand after you sound the note.

"I GOT MY EYES ON YOU"
Buddy Guy

Words and Music by Willie Dixon
and Buddy Guy

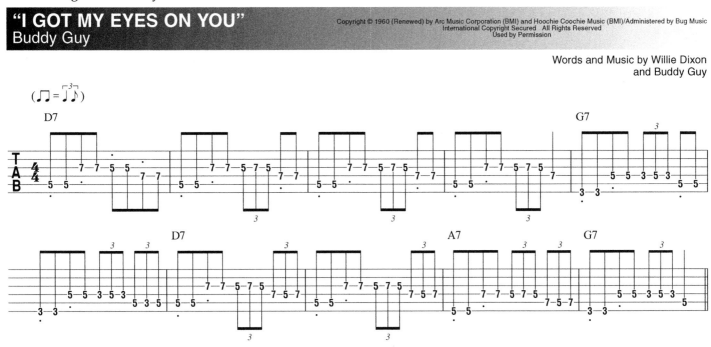

Next up we have the classic opening phrase from "Boom Boom" by the legendary John Lee Hooker. There are quite a few *reverse* slides here that might take some getting used to if you've not tried them before. This is an excellent example of how effective the open-position E blues scale can be, so play it with some feeling!

"BOOM BOOM"
John Lee Hooker

Words and Music by
John Lee Hooker

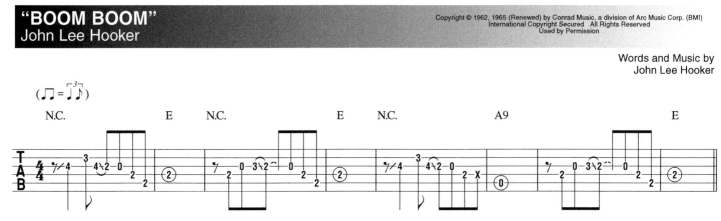

Finally we have a great open-position riff using the A minor pentatonic scale that appears at the start of the classic "I'm Your Hoochie Coochie Man." The most famous version of this song is by Muddy Waters, although Willie Dixon wrote the tune. It's simple but so effective!

"I'M YOUR HOOCHIE COOCHIE MAN"
Muddy Waters

Written by Willie Dixon

BLUES LICKS

In this lesson, we're going to learn about something dear to almost every guitar player's heart: blues licks. For decades now, the guitar's been the instrument of choice in the blues genre, and it's no wonder why. The ability to bend notes, slide around, and achieve all kinds of tones, loud and soft, makes the guitar perfectly suited for this emotionally charged music. In the hands of a seasoned blues veteran, the guitar can scream, cry, growl, whisper, or moan as intensely as any voice.

So let's look at how some of this is done. For simplicity, we'll work exclusively in the key of A for this lesson, but all of these licks can be transposed to any other key just by moving up or down the fretboard.

Many of the licks we'll look at come from the **minor pentatonic scale**, which we covered in great detail in the previous chapter. The licks that follow are primarily based on the A minor pentatonic box fingering (see diagram on page 6). The fingering scheme for the box pattern is as follows: All the fifth-fret notes (on all strings) are played with the index finger, all the seventh-fret notes (on the A, D, and G strings) are played with the ring finger, and all the eighth-fret notes (on the low E, B, and high E strings) are played either with the pinky or ring finger. You'll notice that your DVD instructors each use a different method. Either way is fine, and it wouldn't be a bad idea to practice it both ways, since each way has its own advantages and disadvantages.

If you follow this fingering guideline, the minor pentatonic scale will be a breeze to memorize and play.

Bending Notes

Since blues is so much about inflection, bending notes is very common. You can really bend just about any note of this scale shape, but here are some of the most common bends all based around our A minor pentatonic scale shape.

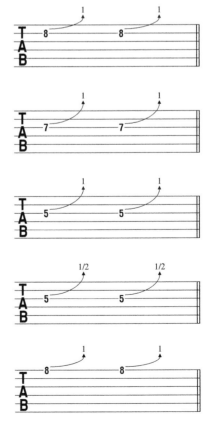

A) The first example shows the flat 7th bending up to the root; that's the note G bending up a whole step to A.

B) The second example shows the 4th bending up to the 5th; that's the note D bending up a whole step to E.

C) The third example shows the flat 3rd bending up to the 4th; that's the note C bending up a whole step to D.

D) The fourth example shows the flat 3rd bending up to the major 3rd; that's the note C bending up just a half step to C♯.

E) The fifth example shows the flat 3rd (played on fret 8 of the high E string) being bent up to the 4th; that's C going up a whole step to D again, just up an octave. You can get loads of energy into this last one!

With all of these bends, make sure you're bending accurately up to the note you're aiming for. If it's a whole-step bend, play the note that's two frets higher up from your starting note. That's the note that your bent note should sound like. So if you're bending from fret 8, your bent note should sound like the note on fret 10. Got it? If it's a half step bend, then you're only going up one fret. Play the note that's one fret higher up from your starting note and make sure your bent note sounds like it.

Let's look at some classic minor pentatonic blues licks. Here's one that's been used by everyone from Chuck Berry to Zakk Wylde. Barre the first two strings with your first finger and hold them down firmly. Dig your 3rd finger into the G string for the bend and go for it.

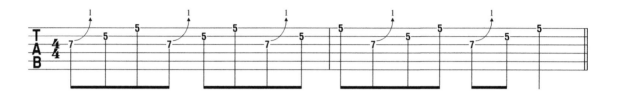

In this next one, we use a quarter-step bend, which is half way up to a half-step bend. It's a subtle effect, but it really adds to the bluesy flavor.

First, here's the lick without the quarter-step bend.

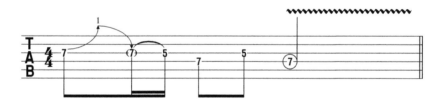

Now we'll add the quarter-step bend on the C note.

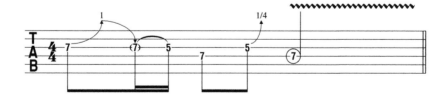

This is subtle, so gently does it and don't dig in too hard. It's not real in-your-face, but you miss it when it's not there. Listen to the example on the DVD carefully here to get the sound in your head.

Ok, that's enough subtly! For this next one, you're going to be adding vibrato to a double stop with your first finger. This is a very Hendrix/Stevie Ray type of sound. Be sure to really dig in to this one.

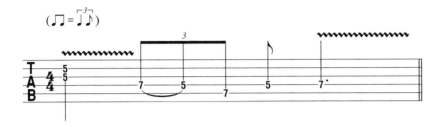

Remember that the blues is all about expression. There are literally dozens of ways to play just about any lick, and they'll all convey a different emotion or attitude. Let's take a look at a simple lick as an example—something like this.

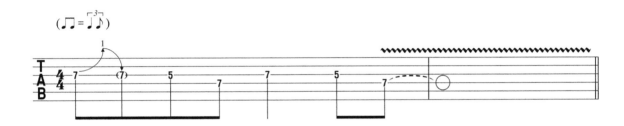

Now with the use of different bends, slides, etc., you can get a whole lot of mileage out of this one lick. Here are just a few ways you might play it. The addition of a slide and a small bend gives us this sound.

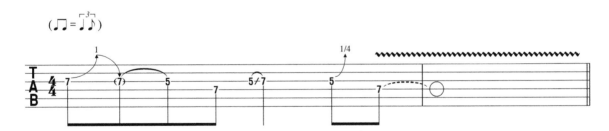

In this next one, we have a slide to kick things off and then a big bend for your first finger to deal with in the middle.

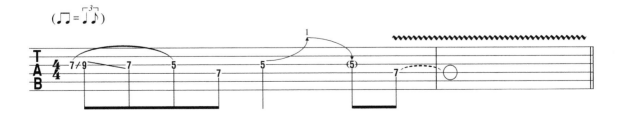

Listen to this next one carefully to get the staccato feel on the notes.

There are a couple of tricky twists on this final variation, including a pre-bend to start with and a position change at the end.

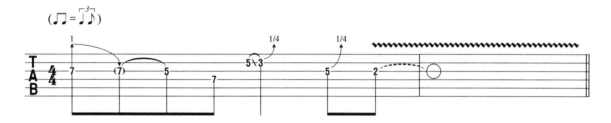

There really is no limit to what you can do so use your imagination. When you combine these ideas with different tones, the use of dynamics, playing with your fingers instead of a pick, and so on, you'll come up with just about endless variations.

Blues Scale Phrases

You may remember from the previous section how adding one note, the ♭5th, can transform a minor pentatonic scale into a blues scale (refer to page 6). It's amazing how the addition of that one note can suddenly change things up! The blues scale sound is very distinct and... well, bluesy. Think about the opening riffs to Cream's "Sunshine of your Love" or Led Zeppelin's "Heartbreaker." *That's* the sound of a blues scale!

To change our A minor pentatonic box shape into a blues scale, just add the E♭ note on the sixth fret of the A string (played with the middle finger) and the eighth fret of the G string (played with the pinky or ring finger). Watch how your DVD instructors finger the E♭ on the 8th fret of the G string. Doug uses his pinky, and Wolf stretches out his ring finger. Try it both ways and see which works better for you.

Remember that the ♭5 note is known as the *blue note*, so you can make your minor pentatonic licks sound even bluesier by adding it in. Try this.

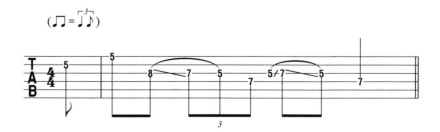

Or how about having the blue note down on the bass strings like this?

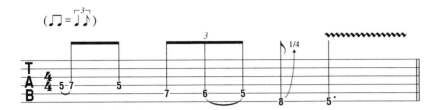

You can also accent the ♭5 blues note with bends and grace notes, as in this next lick. We're back to being subtle again, but it's a great idea.

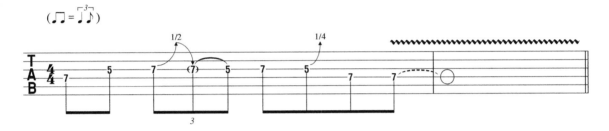

This next one has a cool little backwards slide from the blues note. It's something you might hear Robben Ford play.

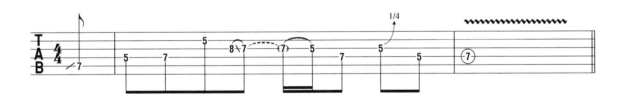

Here's a lick that recreates the classic sound of the Delta blues—not too fast on this one!

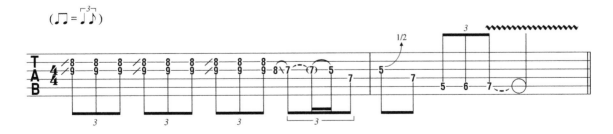

The Major Pentatonic Scale

Another popular scale used in the blues is the major pentatonic scale. This is another five-note scale, but it consists of the root, 2nd, 3rd, 5th, and 6th degrees of the major scale. It sounds much happier than the minor pentatonic.

A major scale		A	B	C#	D	E	F#	G#
		Root	2nd	3rd	4th	5th	6th	7th
A major pentatonic scale		A	B	C#		E	F#	
		Root	2nd	3rd		5th	6th	

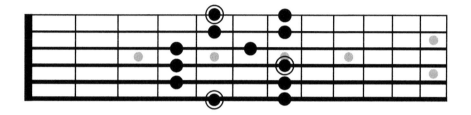

This is a much brighter, sweeter sound and not as tough as the minor pentatonic. Let's look at a few ideas to help get the sound of this scale in your head. Try this one.

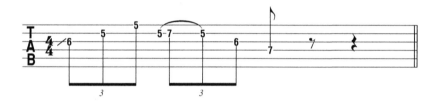

This next little phrase could be used straight after the previous one in a solo.

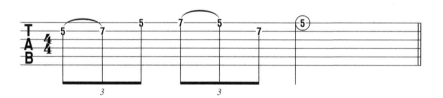

You can get a really nice sound by bending the 2nd up a half step—that's bending from the note B up to C—like in this next lick.

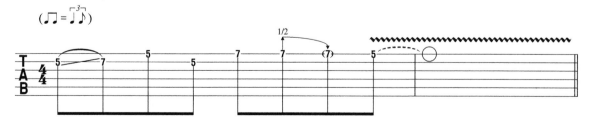

If we play the A major pentatonic scale in a different position, starting up at fret 9, we get the B.B. King box shape.

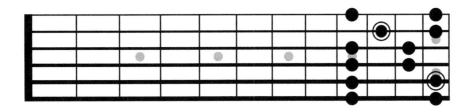

This next idea uses this new shape and combines it with a bend from the 5th to the 6th. We've also moved things up an octave thanks to our new shape. Listen to that sweet B.B. King sound.

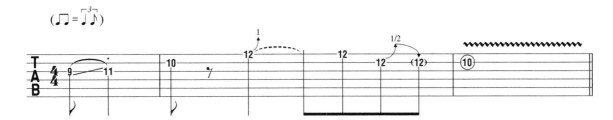

Composite Blues Scale

Of course, a lot of players combine two or all three of these scales at once in common practice. When you combine the minor pentatonic, blues scale, and the major pentatonic, you end up with what's sometimes called the *composite blues scale*. Here it is in the same fifth-fret area.

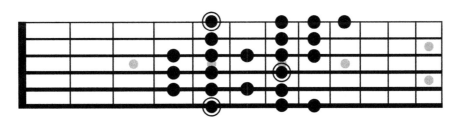

Now this does sound a little unusual, and most people don't really think of this as an actual scale in its own right. They usually think more in terms of combining the other scales that we have been looking at: minor pentatonic, blues, and major pentatonic.

For example, you could start off with the major pentatonic and then move into the blues scale, finishing off major again, like in this next idea.

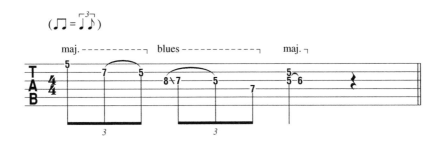

This one starts off with the bright sound of the major pentatonic and then gets really mean with the blues scale.

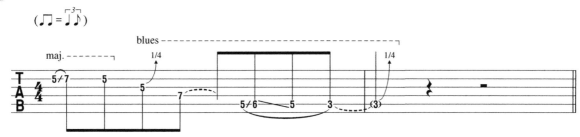

This next one is played in the higher octave and can sound really great. Listen to the tension that's created by combining these scales together.

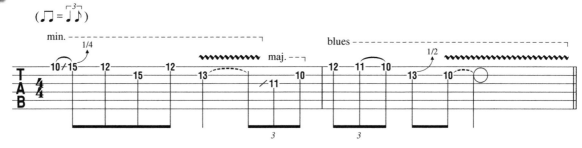

If you want something a little more laid back, try this next one out.

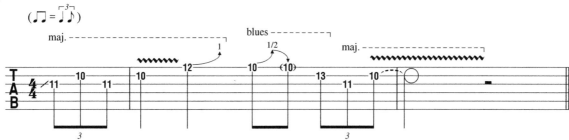

Before we wrap it up for this lesson, let's take a look at some lead phrases taken from tracks of a few of the blues masters. This first one is taken from Robben Ford's version of "Talk to Your Daughter" and features a seamless combination of notes from the G major pentatonic and G blues scales. On the original recording (from the *Talk to Your Daughter* album), you'll find this just before the second verse starts. Very tasty!

Words and Music by J.B. Lenoir
and Alex Atkins

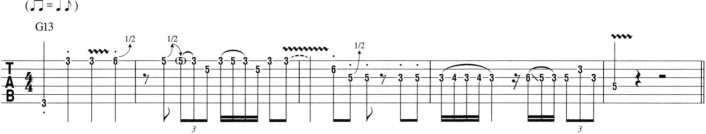

We're staying in the key of G for this next one and sticking mainly to the blues scale, although there's a hint of the major pentatonic. It's taken from the introduction of Stevie Ray Vaughan's "Texas Flood." Dig your fingers in real hard for this one and notice how the D7 chord is sounded at the end of this phrase.

"TEXAS FLOOD"
Stevie Ray Vaughan

Words and Music by Larry Davis
and Joseph W. Scott

Tune down 1/2 step:
(low to high) Eb–Ab–Db–Gb–Bb–Eb

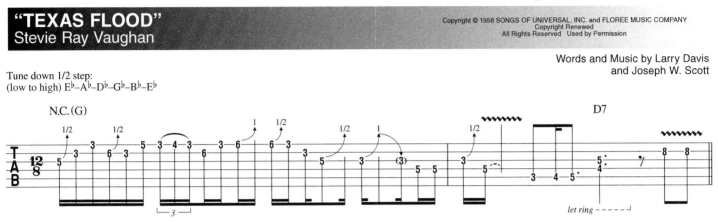

This next phrase shows how much you can do with very few notes and comes courtesy of one of the best blues players at doing just that, B.B. King. We're looking at the introduction to "The Thrill Is Gone". It's in the key of B minor, and the notes are all being played in the box number 2 scale shape you learnt in the Blues Scale chapter. Listen to the track carefully to pick up on the emotion that goes into every note.

"THE THRILL IS GONE"
B.B. King

Words and Music by Roy Hawkins
and Rick Darnell

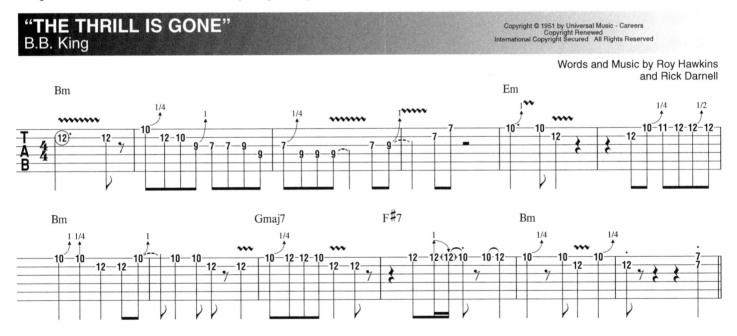

Next up is Albert Collins and a great little phrase taken from the beginning of "Frosty." Collins played with his guitar in open E minor tuning up a half step on this track. I'm thinking you're not gonna fancy re-tuning your guitars like that, so it's written out here in standard tuning. He's using a combination of the D blues and D major pentatonic scales. Watch out for the string bend in bar 4; you're holding down two notes at fret 12 but you're only bending the note on the G string. Keep that B string still!

"FROSTY"
Albert Collins

By Albert Collins

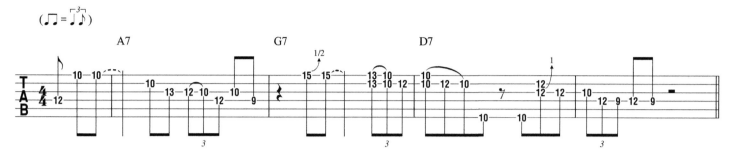

The next phrase is a double-stop, B♭ minor pentatonic lick (with a hint of the major pentatonic) from "Louisiana Bayou Drive" by T-Bone Walker. This is a really useful idea and a great way of creating energy and momentum in your solos, so try and listen to the original track carefully to get the timing.

"LOUISIANA BAYOU DRIVE"
T-Bone Walker

Words and Music by
Aaron "T-Bone" Walker

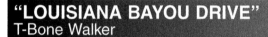

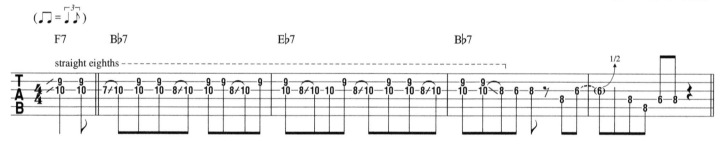

Finally we have Albert King and a short, but quite complex, phrase taken from the opening of "Born Under a Bad Sign." We're using notes from the B minor pentatonic, but there are a load of string bends to deal with here and some quite complex timing.

"BORN UNDER A BAD SIGN"
Albert King

Words and Music by Booker T. Jones
and William Bell

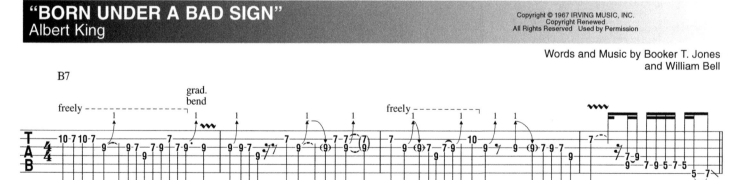

BLUES RHYTHM GUITAR

From boogie to rhumba to slow blues and the shuffle, blues rhythm guitar can be just as fun and varied as playing lead. We're going to take a look here at many of the different ways to play blues rhythm guitar.

To study the blues is to study the very roots of American popular music. The blues is part of practically every genre, from jazz to bluegrass, and from rock to reggae. So having a solid understanding of the blues will help you in understanding many forms of music.

Shuffle or Swing Feel

One of the most important aspects of blues rhythm is known as the *shuffle*, or *swing feel*. We touched on this a bit earlier; this is where eighth notes are played unevenly.

For the shuffle feel, the beat is subdivided into three parts (triplets), and eighth notes are played as the first and third triplet, which creates an uneven, "long-short" sound to the eighth notes.

When a shuffle feel is desired, you'll see this symbol (♫ = ♪♪) at the start of a piece of music.

When you play eighth notes the normal way, which is called playing with a straight feel, the eighth notes have an even feel. You can hear this on the DVD.

The next example on the DVD demonstrates the same eighth notes being played with a shuffle feel.

(♫ = ♪♪)

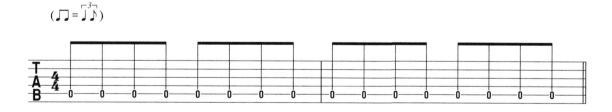

It has a kind of "galloping" sound to it that really helps drive the music along. Notice from the above examples that they are both written out in almost exactly the same way. The only difference is that the shuffle feel notes have the shuffle symbol included at the start. Once you've heard this shuffle feel, it's pretty easy to play, and you've probably heard it used in countless songs. You do need to stay nice and relaxed as you're playing this however, so keep listening to it carefully and make sure you've got it nailed before you move on!

Seventh Chords

Before we put the shuffle to use, let's talk about chords. Basic blues progressions consist of three chords: the I, IV, and V chords.

These are derived from the first, fourth, and fifth degrees of the major scale. So if we're in the key of A, the I chord would be A, the IV chord would be D, and the V chord would be E.

A	B	C#	D	E	F#	G#	A
1	2	3	4	5	6	7	1

To take this a step further, blues harmony often includes *seventh* chords instead of just major chords. With a *dominant* seventh chord, we add a flat 7th (♭7th) to the major triad. This means that an A dominant seventh chord (A7) contains the following notes.

A dominant seventh chord (A7)	**A**	**C#**	**E**	**G**
	Root	3rd	5th	♭7th

Don't worry if this doesn't make much sense at the moment! We're here to play the blues; and while we could spend the rest of this lesson just discussing the music theory behind all of this, where would you rather be: onstage or at the library? For now it's good enough to just recognize and remember the I–IV–V chord idea.

12-Bar Shuffle

Another important blues element is the 12-bar progression. This is the most common blues form. Let's check it out in the key of A. Remember to play this using the shuffle feel and to use our I, IV, and V chords.

Here's the A7 chord.

The D7 chord.

And the E7 chord.
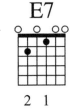

Now let's strum this 12-bar blues with alternating down-and-up strokes. Listen to the track carefully to get that shuffle feel nice and relaxed.

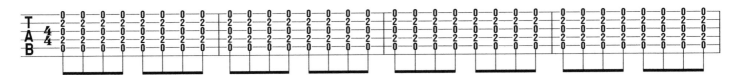

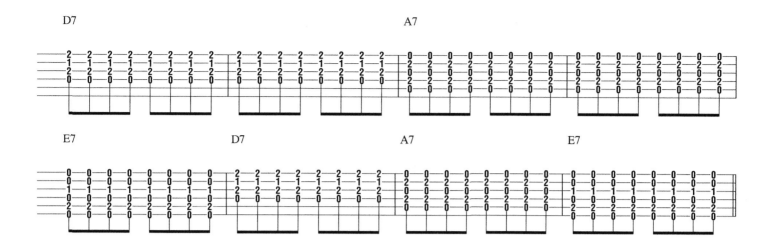

Once you're happy with that, let's try playing it again, but this time we'll add in a few extras. In measure 2 we'll add the IV chord for just that one measure. This is called a "quick change." And in the last two bars we'll add what is called a "turnaround" with a I–IV–I–V chord change. Let's play it in A again, but now we'll play it with barre chords.

 Here's the A7 barre chord. 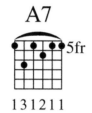 Here's the D7 barre chord. 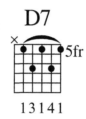 And, finally, the E7 barre chord.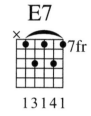

 And here's our 12-bar blues with the quick change and the turnaround added in.

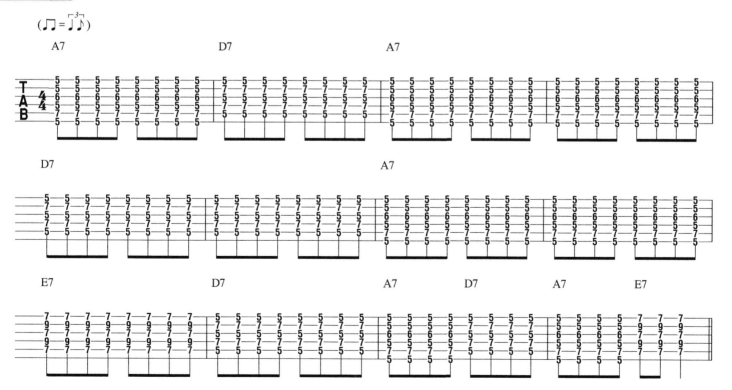

If you're not comfortable with barre chords yet, then just stick to playing both these 12-bar blues using your open chord shapes; they'll still sound great!

Shuffle Patterns

Many players will use shuffle patterns, where 5th chords (also known as *power* chords) are alternated with 6th chords. This can be a lot of fun to play as it adds some movement to the progression.

Let's play our 12-bar blues in A again, but now with an open-position shuffle pattern. The last two bars have a turnaround variation just to make things a little more interesting. It's common to play this with all downstrokes, but you can also try alternating.

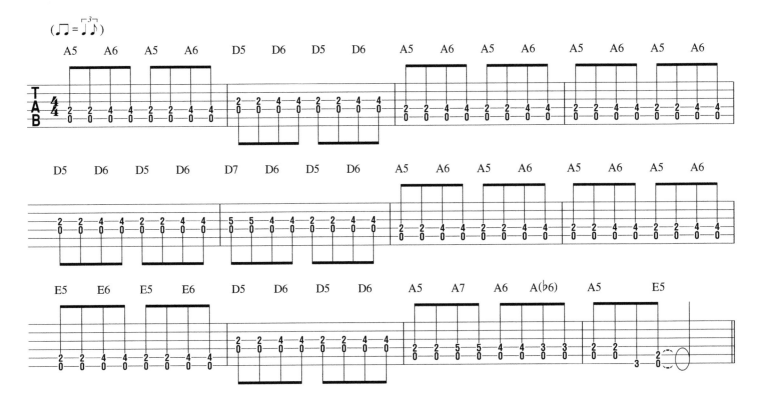

Make sure you practice the individual patterns in each measure on their own first before you worry too much about changing from one set of strings to the next. Take time to ensure you're only striking the pair of strings that you need for each one and make sure you've got that shuffle feel!

Now let's try a blues shuffle in a moveable position in the key of G. The basic chords we're using here are G (the I chord), C (the IV chord), and D (the V chord). Here you'll have to stretch your pinky to play the 6th chords. Keep your fingers arched over the fretboard and anchor your thumb on the back of the neck. If you've not tried this before, then easy does it, as the stretch can take some getting used to. Check out the DVD to see how this is done if you're not sure.

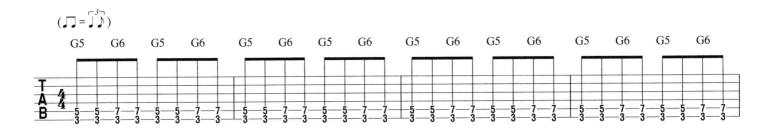

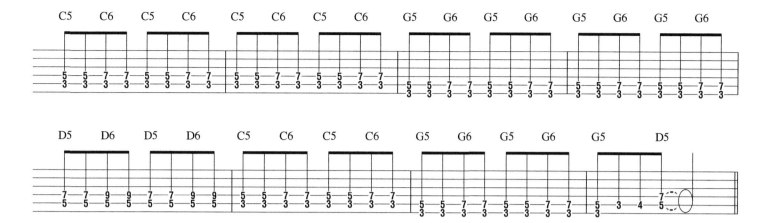

Before we leave these shuffle patterns, here's one more for you to try. We're back in open position in the key of A for this one, but there are a couple of little changes thrown in for a bit of variety along the way. Enjoy!

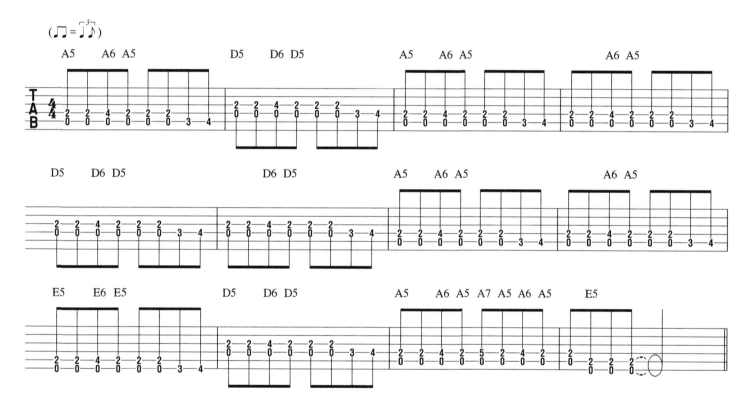

Boogie Patterns

Boogie patterns are based on single-note repeating riffs rather than chords or a shuffle pattern. Let's play a basic boogie in E. We're still following our standard 12-bar blues progression, but we'll now play it in the key of E. The chords in this key are E7 (the I chord), A7 (the IV chord), and B7 (the V chord). The DVD shows this being played at a medium tempo. Once you've got the hang of it at this speed, you should try it at quicker tempos as well, which can give it more of a rockabilly feel. But make sure you can play it slowly first!

Use alternate picking, or down-and-up picking for this one. You'll have to shift your fretting-hand position slightly and stretch your pinky for the B7 chord change as we lose all those open strings. Here it is.

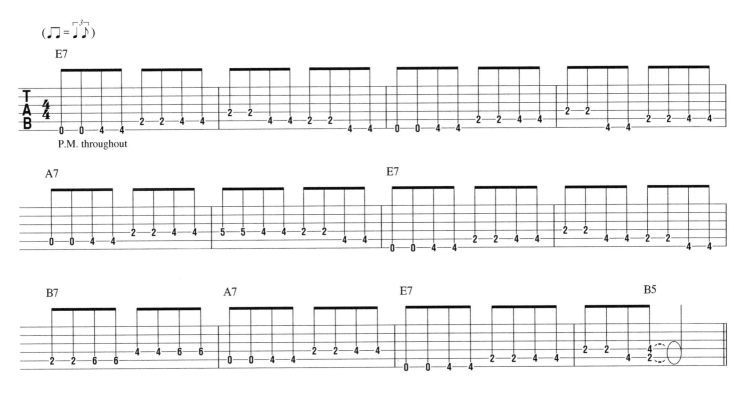

 Here's another cool one, in the key of A this time. Use alternate picking here as well, and it will roll along nicely. There's quite a bit of jumping around between different strings on this one, so practice it slowly at first.

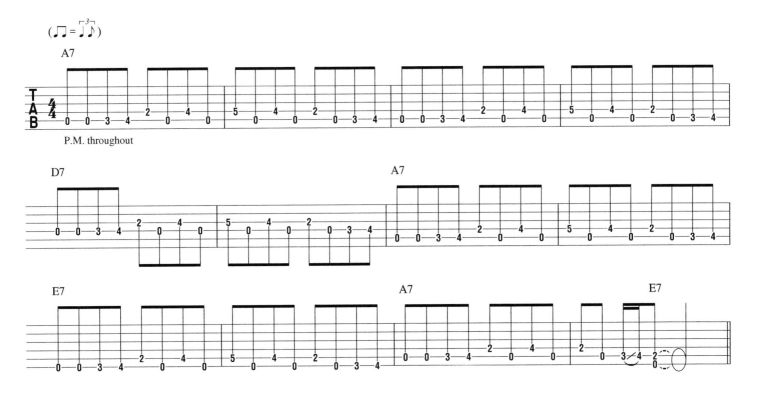

And now let's try this one, which is also in A. We're not using any open strings for this one, so it might not be as easy as the previous examples; take your time. If you check out the DVD, you'll hear this being played at quite a speed, so aim for that once you've got the hang of it at a slower tempo!

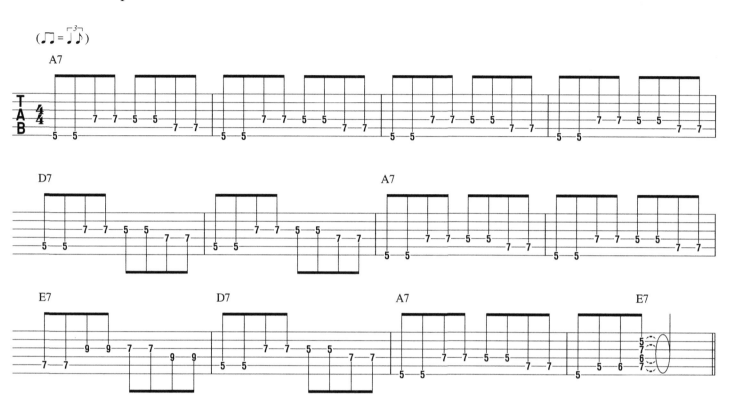

Rhumba Blues

Not all blues is played with a shuffle feel. The *rhumba* is a Cuban rhythm heard in New Orleans-style blues that uses straight eighth notes.

This rhumba contains a single-note line in the key of A.

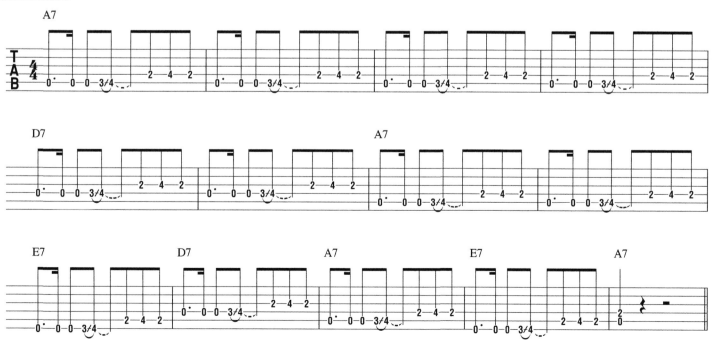

31

Ninth Chords

Next let's talk about a common blues chord called the *ninth chord*. A ninth chord is a dominant seventh chord with a 9th added. The 9th is the same note as the 2nd, just an octave up. An A9 would contain these notes:

A ninth chord (A9)	A	C♯	E	G	B
	Root	3rd	5th	♭7th	9th

One common moveable blues chord shape for the ninth chord looks like this, an E9 for example, rooted on the 5th string.

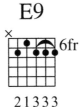

And here's a shape we can use that's rooted on the 6th string. This one's A9.

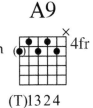

Let's put our new chords to use in this next blues in A where we'll slide the upper notes of each ninth chord. Keep pressure on the strings when you slide so the notes ring out.

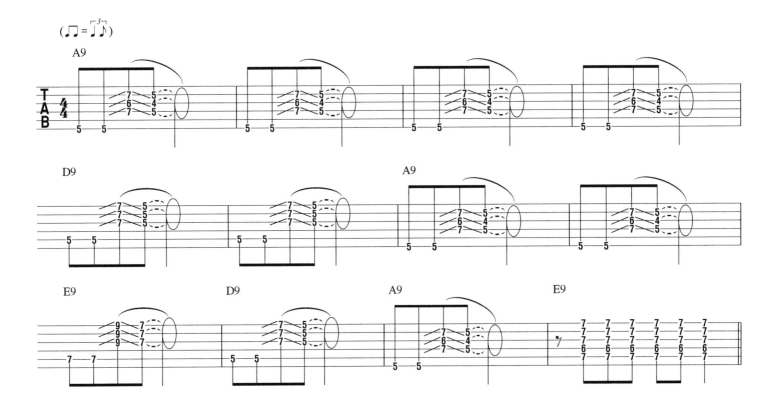

It's a really cool and tasteful way to play the blues—very much in the style of T-Bone Walker.

Now that you've got the hang of those ninth chord shapes, let's try something that you might hear in a big band setting played by someone like B.B. King. This works well at both slower and faster tempos; just make sure you keep your strumming hand nice and relaxed.

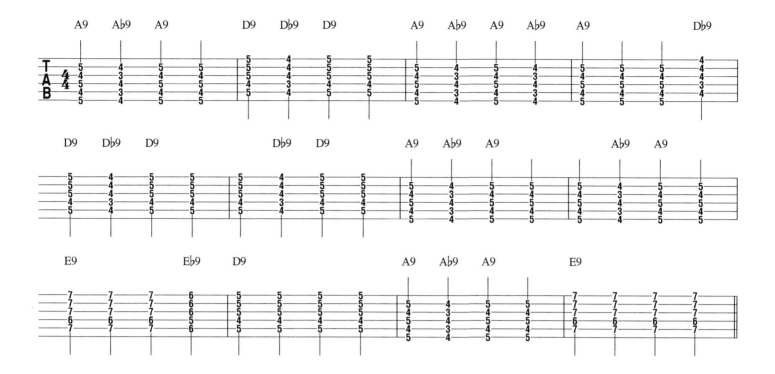

Mixing Rhythm and Lead

Most often there is only one guitarist in a blues band, so he or she will often switch between playing rhythm and lead parts. You'll hear a common blues-ism known as "call and response," in which the vocalist will sing a line and answer it with a similar lick on the guitar. B.B. King comes to mind as one who does this often.

The final example on this segment of the DVD shows a slow blues arrangement that mixes rhythm and lead parts.

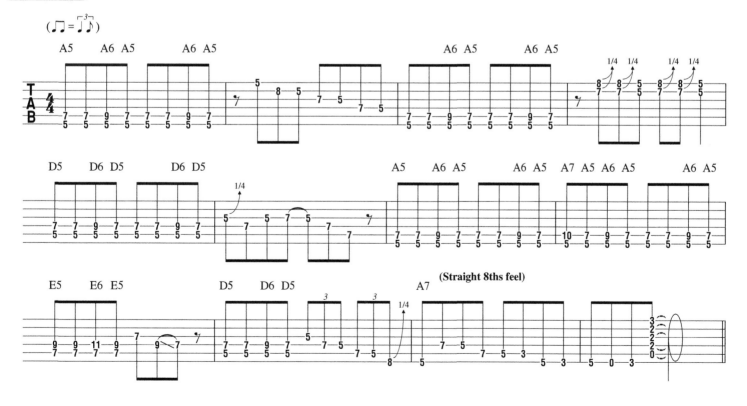

You should be okay with the rhythm parts on this one since you've played those shuffle patterns, in the key of G, earlier. Learn each lead line individually and put it together a chunk at a time. Just because it's slow doesn't mean it's easy!

To close this chapter, let's look at how some of these ideas have been used in some songs. First up we have an excerpt from the rhythm of "Tell Me" as played by Stevie Ray Vaughan. It's a shuffle pattern in the key of C, but watch out for the open-string notes and the damped chord where the plectrum rakes quickly across the strings—classic Stevie Ray!

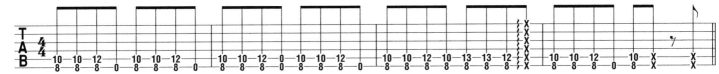

Words and Music by
Chester Burnett

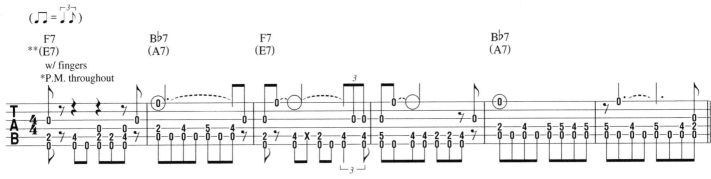

We couldn't look at the blues and not have some Robert Johnson, so here goes. This is taken from the opening verse of "Sweet Home Chicago" and is notated in open position. To play along with the original recording, you'll need to use a capo on the first fret. You'll also need to pluck the strings with your fingers or use a combination of plectrum and fingers to catch all the notes. Take your time here, as this ain't easy.

"SWEET HOME CHICAGO"
Robert Johnson

Words and Music by
Robert Johnson

*Downstemmed notes only.
**Symbols in parentheses represent chord names respective to capoed guitar.
Symbols above reflect actual sounding chords. Capoed fret is "0" in TAB.

Next we have a great example of chord playing using 7th and 9th chords as featured on the Albert Collins'
track "Collins' Mix." The chords are following the horn section, so keep the rhythm nice and tight and make
sure your strings are silent where the rests are indicated.

"COLLINS' MIX"
Albert Collins

By Albert Collins

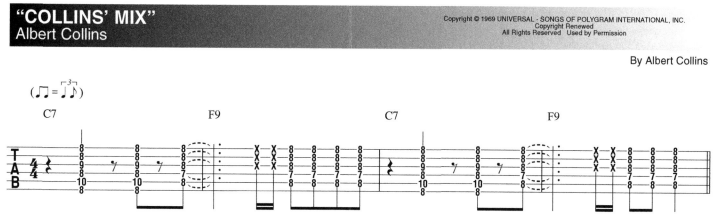

This next one shows what you can do when you combine a shuffle pattern with some chords. It's taken from
the Elmore James track "Dust My Broom" and has been arranged for standard tuning (the original is in open
D tuning). You have to jump around the neck of the guitar a little here to get from the D chord shape to the
shuffle pattern, but it's worth the effort.

"DUST MY BROOM"
Elmore James

Words and Music by Elmore James
and Robert Johnson

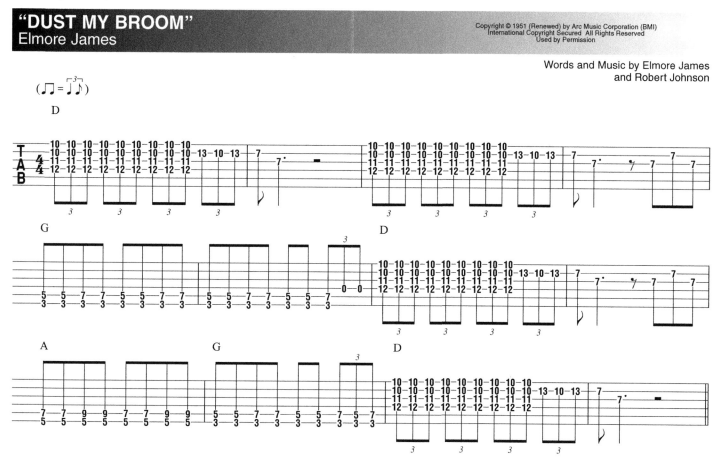

Finally, we have a great idea based on a shuffle pattern but with the notes played individually rather than as a chord. It's taken from the track "Talkin' Woman" by Lowell Fulsom, and you'll also hear a similar idea played on the Albert Collins' version of this track. You have some big stretches to make here; jumping from fret 8 to fret 3 is physically demanding, so easy does it at first.

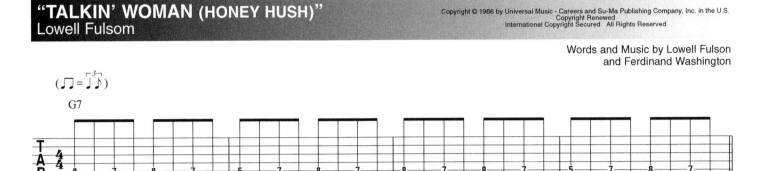

"TALKIN' WOMAN (HONEY HUSH)"
Lowell Fulsom

Words and Music by Lowell Fulson
and Ferdinand Washington

let ring throughout

BLUES TURNAROUNDS

If you're a serious blues player, you've obviously got plenty of licks in your bag of tricks. But one type of lick in particular, that's almost solely applicable in 12-bar blues, is for some reason often neglected. It's called the *turnaround*.

In this chapter we're going to focus on learning some of these crucial two-measure phrases that no true blues man, or woman, should be without.

12-Bar Blues Progression

The turnaround occurs during measures 11 through 12 of a standard 12-bar blues. Its purpose is to "turn" the progression around and set it back up for the next chorus. For instance, in the key of E, we'd have the following chords for a standard 12-bar blues:

|| **E7** | **E7** | **E7** | **E7** |

| **A7** | **A7** | **E7** | **E7** |

| **B7** | **A7** | **E7** | **B7** ||

There are tons of variations on the blues turnaround but, with the exception of some jazz blues, they pretty much all share two common elements:

They begin on the I chord
They end on the V chord.

In the above example, the I chord is the E7, and the V chord is the B7. Now there are plenty of ways to get from one to the other, as we'll soon see, but those are the parameters within which we'll work.

We'll look at some turnarounds in both electric and acoustic styles in this lesson, and we'll start with electric.

Electric-Style Turnarounds

One of the most common blues played on the electric guitar is the shuffle in E. Just think of "Sweet Home Chicago," "Hideaway," "Pride & Joy," etc. Playing in the key of E allows the use of lots of open strings, which comes in handy for turnarounds.

Open-Position Turnarounds

Let's take a look at some classic turnaround moves in this style. Here's our first lick—something Stevie Ray might have played.

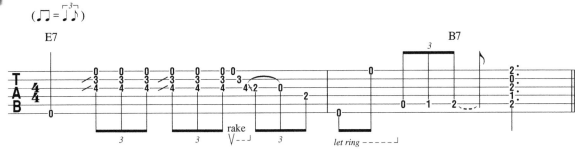

At the end of the first measure, there's a *reverse rake*. To do this, you drag the pick in a single motion up across the top three strings. This can be quite tricky if you haven't done it before so check out the DVD to see it demonstrated clearly and slowly.

There are lots of variations on this classic lick. Let's take a look at some. Here's our first variation.

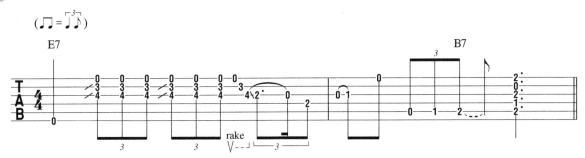

So we stuck pretty close to the original; we just altered the rhythm a bit on the rake lick and added a bluesy little minor-to-major 3rd move in the second measure.

Here's our second variation.

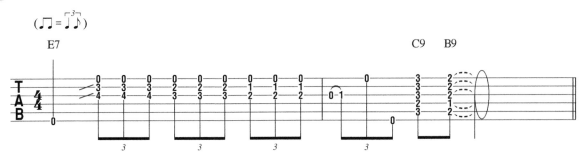

In this one we're adding some chromatic motion by moving the same shape down in the first measure. In the second measure, we're anticipating the B9 chord from a half step above. These ideas use notes that are outside our key of E, which create a nice musical tension that makes the resolution really satisfying.

This third variation is a similar idea to the previous one. We're thinning out the chromatic descent in measure 1 to two notes and playing the notes one by one rather than as a chord. Magic Sam used to play something like this.

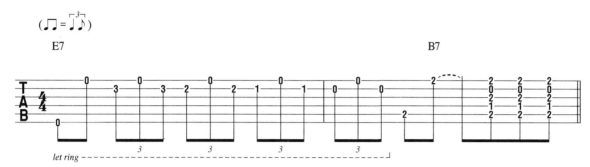

Once you've nailed the first lick and the three variations, try varying it a little yourself and see what you come up with.

Ok, let's look at our next lick for the shuffle in E. This one's a little more typical of Muddy Waters.

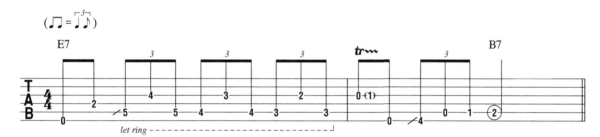

This is another chromatically descending move but with a completely different sound from the previous turn-arounds. In measure 1 we're descending in 6ths this time instead of 3rds. Let's not get too wrapped up with the theory here; just know that the interval between the two different notes in each triplet here is called a 6th. Make sure you keep two fingers in place for the notes in each triplet so that the notes ring into each other. We're also adding a trill in measure 2 by hammering on and pulling off on fret 1—another classic device found in many turnarounds.

For our first variation on this lick, we're strumming the 6ths and letting the open first and second strings ring throughout. This creates some beautiful blues dissonances. Make sure the D string is muted out while you're strumming the 6ths. The underside of your second finger should be able to take care of this.

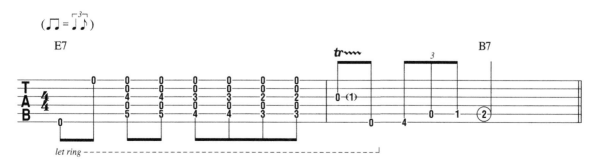

In this next variation we're arpeggiating through the descent again, but including the open E string as the third note in each triplet. This variation has a few minor differences from the previous variations—the trill is gone (no, not B.B. King's "The Thrill Is Gone"), and a descending pentatonic lick is used at the end of the lick, rather than the bass run. Also, notice that we end on the note A, which is the ♭7th of the B7 chord, rather than the root. You might want to try this one with different pick-hand approaches: using a pick throughout, your pick and fingers, or maybe just your fingers. It'll sound great whichever you choose. Because this one requires a bit more precision, it's usually played at a slightly slower tempo.

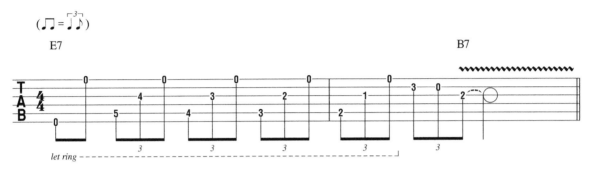

Non Open-Position Turnrounds

Turnarounds tend to be a bit less complicated when open strings aren't involved. In these cases, more single notes are used, and harmonies are often implied rather than actually sounded. Since no open strings are involved, you can easily move these to any key. We'll work in the key of C for these next ideas.

First off is a great lick in the style of blues pioneer T-Bone Walker.

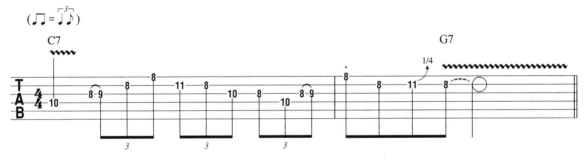

Notice the mixing of major and minor 3rds that we get by hammering on from fret 8 to fret 9 on the G string. Otherwise, it's mostly C minor pentatonic. The 5th, G, is carefully targeted at the end to coincide with the arrival of the V chord (G7).

Here's our first variation on this lick. We add a climactic bend on the high E string in measure 1 before coming back down the scale. Make sure you don't bend those notes too far.

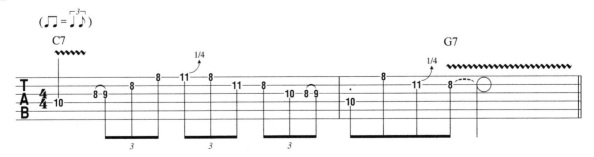

In this next variation, we're descending down a Dorian/blues hybrid scale and finishing off with a bass run up to the G. We've also got another hammer-on from the minor 3rd to major 3rd in the second measure.

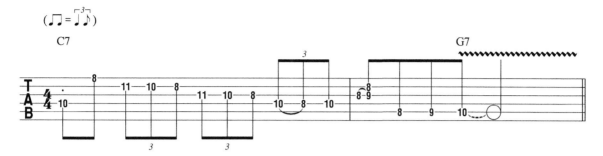

Sometimes it can be really effective to use only a small selection of notes.

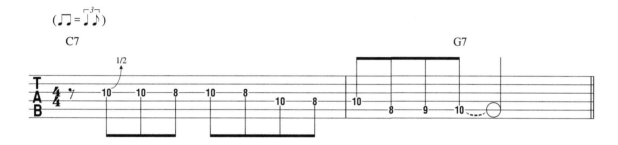

And here's another neat little idea that's based on one of the open-position E turnarounds we looked at earlier but played without any open strings in the key of C again.

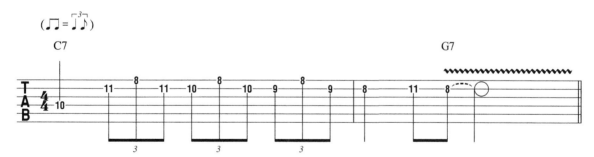

Acoustic-Style Turnarounds

Ok, now it's time to get down with some more country old-time blues on acoustic. Although open tunings were used by many players in this style, we're gonna stick to standard tuning here. We'll even arrange a few open-tuning turnarounds for standard tuning.

We'll be playing fingerstyle for most of these examples, but you could use a thumbpick if you prefer. Let's learn some classic turnarounds in G, which allows us some open strings again. Although these would often be played in open G tuning, we can manage in standard tuning just fine.

This one can also be played on the electric guitar, but it sounds particularly nice on acoustic. Notice the staccato feel that this turnaround has and watch your fingering in the second measure to make sure you land on the D7 chord cleanly. Listen to it carefully to get that feel just right.

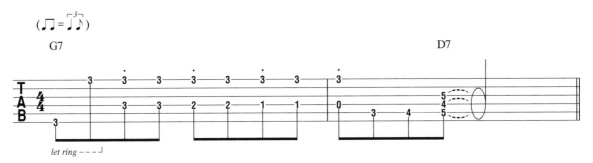

For this next one we're just bringing the pedal G note down an octave so it's played on the open G string.

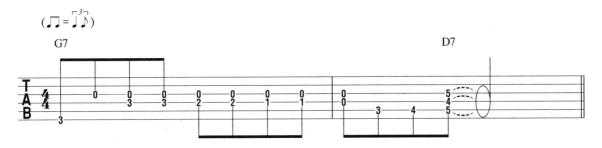

And here's a really pretty variation on this lick. We're bringing in notes on the B string during the descent and arpeggiating against the high G pedal note that's played on fret 3 of the high E string. The right-hand part can be a little tricky on this one, so make sure you play it slowly and evenly until you're comfortable and it sounds good.

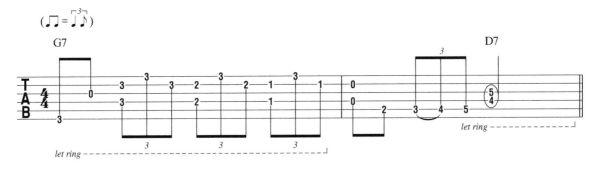

You'll have to be careful with the fingering on your fretting hand for this next one. Use your ring finger to play the note on fret 3 of string 1 and use the remaining fingers to catch the ascending bass notes. Try to let the notes ring into each other.

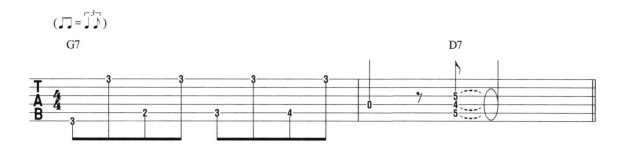

Ok now let's take a fingerstyle acoustic approach to the key of E.

This next lick is pretty much "Fingerstyle blues 101." It's been used in some form by everyone from Robert Johnson to Jimi Hendrix. Again you have to watch your fingering at the end to make sure all of those notes ring out clearly.

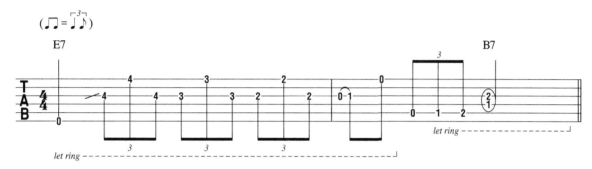

And here's a strummy variation of that one using the ringing open B string as a drone. There are some nice dissonances in the middle of the descent.

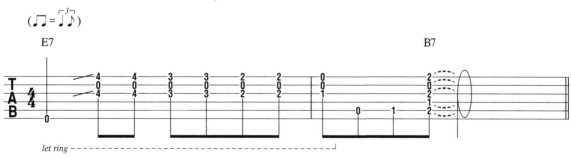

And here we're pedalling the open high E against arpeggiated descending notes on strings 2 and 3. This gives us some more of that great chromatic tension that we heard earlier on with the electric styles.

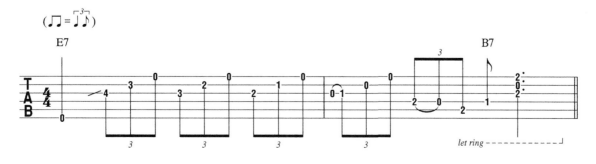

Let's expand our repertoire further by looking at how the blues greats played their turnarounds. First, we have "Sweet Home Chicago" by Robert Johnson, which features a great open-position turnaround in the key of E. You've already played similar ideas to this in the previous examples, but the subtlety of this phrase makes things just a little more complex.

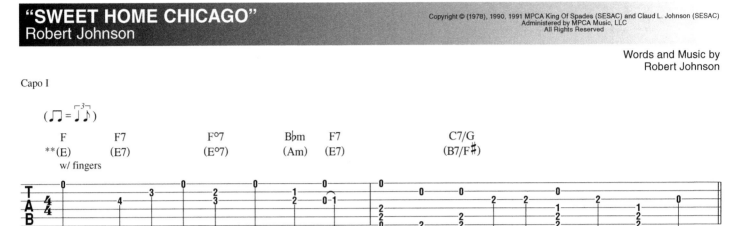

"SWEET HOME CHICAGO"
Robert Johnson

Words and Music by
Robert Johnson

**Symbols in parentheses represent chord names respective to capoed guitar.
Symbols above reflect actual sounding chords. Capoed fret is "0" in TAB.

This next one also includes some similar ideas but is played a lot faster! Notice that Stevie's guitar is tuned down to E♭ on the original track. This is one of the turnarounds that caps off a verse in Stevie Ray Vaughan's classic "Pride And Joy."

"PRIDE AND JOY"
Stevie Ray Vaughan

Written by Stevie Ray Vaughan

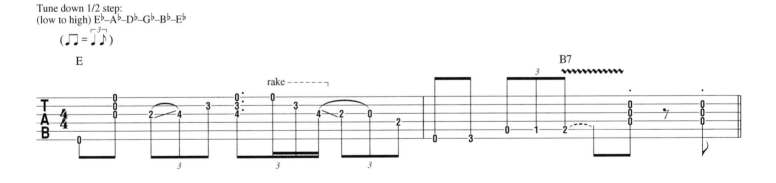

Here's a different approach now from Robben Ford's track "Cannonball Shuffle." This turnaround is in the key of A and has a descending line played on the D string against a ringing A pedal note played on the high E string.

"CANNONBALL SHUFFLE"
Robben Ford

Written by Robben Ford

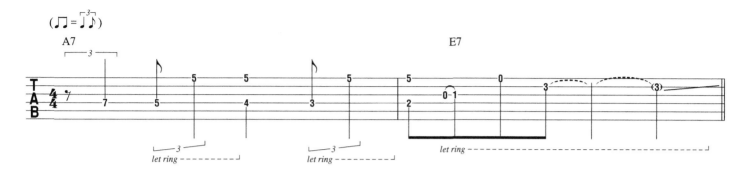

Let's look at a couple of ideas that imply the harmonies as we looked at earlier in this chapter. Have a look at this slow blues turnaround from Buddy Guy's version of "Five Long Years." It's a lovely phrase that uses a C blues scale to give you all the harmonies you need.

"FIVE LONG YEARS"
Buddy Guy

Words and Music by
Eddie Boyd

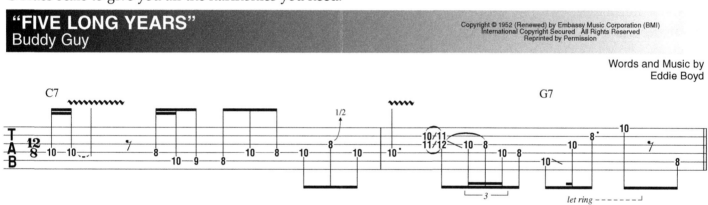

Last up, B.B. King and Eric Clapton teamed up for this rendition of "Three O'Clock Blues" filled with some great phrases throughout. Here's one of Clapton's turnarounds using a combination of the B blues and B major pentatonic scales.

"THREE O'CLOCK BLUES"
B.B. King and Eric Clapton

Words and Music by B.B. King
and Jules Bihari

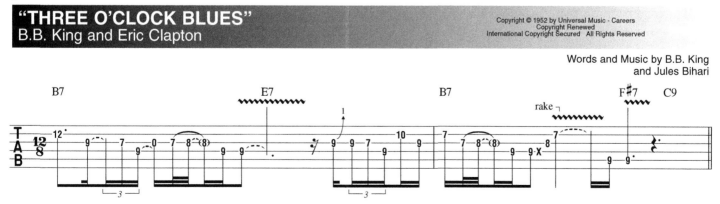

Rhythm Tab Legend

Rhythm Tab is a form of notation that adds rhythmic values to the traditional tab staff.

TABLATURE graphically represents the guitar fingerboard. Each horizontal line represents a string, and each number represents a fret. Rhythmic values are shown using ovals, stems, and dots.

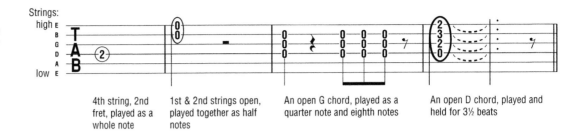

| 4th string, 2nd fret, played as a whole note | 1st & 2nd strings open, played together as half notes | An open G chord, played as a quarter note and eighth notes | An open D chord, played and held for 3½ beats |

Definitions for Special Guitar Notation

HALF-STEP BEND: Strike the note and bend up 1/2 step.

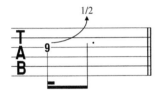

WHOLE-STEP BEND: Strike the note and bend up one step.

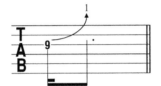

GRACE NOTE BEND: Strike the note and immediately bend up as indicated.

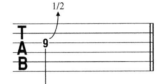

SLIGHT (MICROTONE) BEND: Strike the note and bend up 1/4 step.

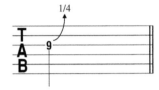

BEND AND RELEASE: Strike the note and bend up as indicated, then release back to the original note. Only the first note is struck.

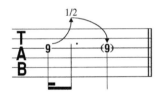

PRE-BEND: Bend the note as indicated, then strike it.

PRE-BEND AND RELEASE: Bend the note as indicated. Strike it and release the bend back to the original note.

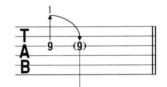

UNISON BEND: Strike the two notes simultaneously and bend the lower note up to the pitch of the higher.

HOLD BEND: While sustaining bent note, strike note on different string.

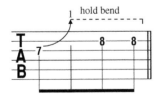

VIBRATO: The string is vibrated by rapidly bending and releasing the note with the fretting hand.

WIDE VIBRATO: The pitch is varied to a greater degree by vibrating with the fretting hand.

HAMMER-ON: Strike the first (lower) note with one finger, then sound the higher note (on the same string) with another finger by fretting it without picking.

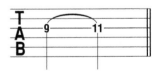

PULL-OFF: Place both fingers on the notes to be sounded. Strike the first note and without picking, pull the finger off to sound the second (lower) note.

HAMMER FROM NOWHERE: Sound note(s) by hammering with fret hand finger only.

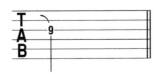

GRACE NOTE SLUR: Strike the note and immediately hammer-on (or pull-off) as indicated.

GRACE NOTE SLUR (CLUSTER): Strike the notes and immediately hammer-on (or pull-off) as indicated.

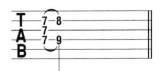

LEGATO SLIDE: Strike the first note and then slide the same fret-hand finger up or down to the second note. The second note is not struck.

SHIFT SLIDE: Same as legato slide, except the second note is struck.

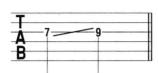

TRILL: Very rapidly alternate between the notes indicated by continuously hammering on and pulling off.

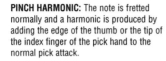

TAPPING: Hammer ("tap") the fret indicated with the pick-hand index or middle finger and pull off to the note fretted by the fret hand.

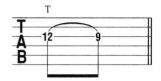

NATURAL HARMONIC: Strike the note while the fret-hand lightly touches the string directly over the fret indicated.

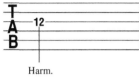

Harm.

PINCH HARMONIC: The note is fretted normally and a harmonic is produced by adding the edge of the thumb or the tip of the index finger of the pick hand to the normal pick attack.

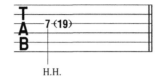

P.H.

HARP HARMONIC: The note is fretted normally and a harmonic is produced by gently resting the pick hand's index finger directly above the indicated fret (in parentheses) while the pick hand's thumb or pick assists by plucking the appropriate string.

H.H.

PICK SCRAPE: The edge of the pick is rubbed down (or up) the string, producing a scratchy sound.

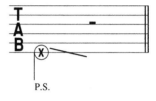

P.S.

MUFFLED STRINGS: A percussive sound is produced by laying the fret hand across the string(s) without depressing, and striking them with the pick hand.

PALM MUTING: The note is partially muted by the pick hand lightly touching the string(s) just before the bridge.

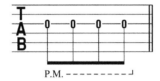

P.M. - - - - - - - - ⌐

RAKE: Drag the pick across the strings indicated with a single motion.

rake - - ⌐

TREMOLO PICKING: The note is picked as rapidly and continuously as possible.

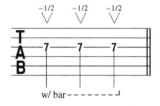

ARPEGGIATE: Play the notes of the chord indicated by quickly rolling them from bottom to top.

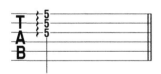

VIBRATO BAR DIVE AND RETURN: The pitch of the note or chord is dropped a specified number of steps (in rhythm), then returned to the original pitch.

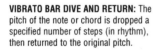

w/ bar -1

VIBRATO BAR SCOOP: Depress the bar just before striking the note, then quickly release the bar.

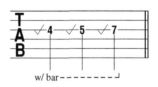

w/ bar - - - - - - - ⌐

VIBRATO BAR DIP: Strike the note and then immediately drop a specified number of steps, then release back to the original pitch.

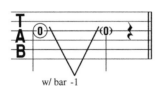

w/ bar - - - - - - ⌐

Additional Musical Definitions

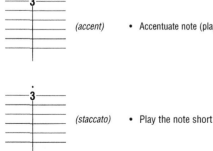

(accent) • Accentuate note (play it louder)

(staccato) • Play the note short

(fermata) • A hold or pause

⊓ • Downstroke

V • Upstroke

• Repeat measures between signs

NOTE: Tablature numbers in parentheses are used when:
• The note is sustained, but a new articulation begins (such as a hammer-on, pull-off, slide, or bend), or
• A bend is released.

MASTER THE *Blues*

12-Bar Blues
by Dave Rubin

The term "12-bar blues" has become synonymous with blues music and is the basis for other forms of popular music. This book is devoted to providing guitarists with all the technical tools necessary for playing 12-bar blues with authority. Covers: boogie, shuffle, swing, riff, and jazzy blues progressions; Chicago, minor, slow, bebop, and other blues styles; soloing, intros, turnarounds, and more.
00695187 Book/Online Audio..............$19.99

75 Blues Turnarounds
by Michael DoCampo with Toby Wine

This book/audio pack teaches 75 turnarounds over common chord progressions in a variety of styles, including those of blues guitar greats like Albert King, Johnny Winter, Mike Bloomfield, Duane Allman, Jeff Beck, T-Bone Walker and others.
02501043 Book/Online Audio..............$14.99

100 Blues Lessons
Guitar Lesson Goldmine
by John Heussenstamm and Chad Johnson

A huge variety of blues guitar styles and techniques are covered, including: turnarounds, hammer-ons and pull-offs, slides, the blues scale, 12-bar blues, double stops, muting techniques, hybrid picking, fingerstyle blues, and much more!
00696452 Book/Online Audio..............$24.99

101 Must-Know Blues Licks
by Wolf Marshall

Now you can add authentic blues feel and flavor to your playing! Here are 101 definitive licks – plus a demonstration CD – from every major blues guitar style, neatly organized into easy-to-use categories. They're all here, including Delta blues, jump blues, country blues, Memphis blues, Texas blues, West Coast blues, Chicago blues, and British blues.
00695318 Book/Online Audio..............$19.99

Beginning Blues Guitar
by Dave Rubin

From B.B. King and Buddy Guy to Eric Clapton and Stevie Ray Vaughan, blues guitar is a constant in American popular music. This book teaches the concepts and techniques fostered by legendary blues guitar players: 12-bar blues; major & minor pentatonic scales; the blues scale; string bending; licks; double-stops; intros and turnarounds; and more.
00695916 Book/Online Audio..............$12.99

Beginning Fingerstyle Blues Guitar
by Arnie Berle & Mark Galbo

A step-by-step method for learning this rich and powerful style. Takes you from the fundamentals of fingerpicking to five authentic blues tunes. Includes graded exercises, illustrated tips, plus standard notation and tablature.
14003799 Book/CD Pack...................$22.99

Brave New Blues Guitar
by Greg Koch

A kaleidoscopic reinterpretation of 16 blues rock titans is the hallmark of this Greg Koch book with over three hours of online video lessons. It breaks down the styles, techniques, and licks of guitarists including Albert Collins, B.B. King, Eric Clapton, Jimi Hendrix, Stevie Ray Vaughan, Johnny Winter and more.
00201987 Book/Online Video............$22.99

Chicago Blues Rhythm Guitar
by Bob Margolin & Dave Rubin

This definitive instructional guitar book features loads of rhythm guitar playing examples to learn and practice, covering a variety of styles, techniques, tips, historical anecdotes, and much more. To top it off, every playing example in the book is performed on the accompanying DVD by Bob Margolin himself!
00121575 Book/DVD Pack.................$22.99

Everything About Playing the Blues
by Wilbur Savidge

An ideal reference guide to playing the blues for all guitarists. Full instruction on blues theory, chords, rhythm, scales, advanced solo technique, beginnings and endings, riff construction and more. Includes play-along audio with 12 jam tracks.
14010625 Book/Online Audio $29.99

Fretboard Roadmaps – Blues Guitar
by Fred Sokolow

Fretboard patterns are roadmaps that all great blues guitarists know and use. This book teaches how to: play lead and rhythm anywhere on the fretboard; play a variety of lead guitar styles; play chords and progressions anywhere on the fretboard, in any key; expand chord vocabulary; learn to think musically, the way the pros do.
00695350 Book/Online Audio..............$15.99

Hal Leonard Blues Guitar Method
by Greg Koch

Real blues songs are used to teach the basics of rhythm and lead blues guitar in the style of B.B. King, Buddy Guy, Eric Clapton, and many others. Lessons include: 12-bar blues; chords, scales and licks; vibrato and string bending; riffs, turnarounds, and boogie patterns; and more!
00697326 Book/Online Audio $19.99

How to Play Blues-Fusion Guitar
by Joe Charupakorn

Study the scales, chords, and arpeggios most commonly used in the blues-fusion style and how to use them in this book. You'll also examine how artists like Matt Schofield, Mike Stern, Scott Henderson, and John Scofield put their own spin on the blues/fusion format.
00137813 Book/Online Audio $19.99

Blues You Can Use Series
by John Ganapes

Blues You Can Use
This comprehensive source for learning blues guitar is designed to develop both your lead and rhythm playing. Blues styles covered include Texas, Delta, R&B, early rock & roll, gospel and blues/rock.
00142420 Book/Online Media.........................$22.99

More Blues You Can Use
This follow up edition covers: pentatonic scales, single-note tremolo, double-string bends, reverse bends, shuffle rhythms, 6th and 9th chords, boogie patterns, chord substitutions, vibrato techniques, and more!
00695165 Book/Online Audio.......................$22.99

Blues Guitar Chords You Can Use
A reference guide to blues, R&B, jazz, and rock rhythm guitar, with hundreds of voicings, chord theory construction, chord progressions and exercises and much more.
00695082...$17.99

Blues Licks You Can Use
Contains music and performance notes for 75 hot lead phrases, covering styles including up-tempo and slow blues, jazz-blues, shuffle blues, swing blues and more!
00695386 Book/Online Audio $17.99

Blues Rhythms You Can Use
Develop your rhythm playing chops with 21 progressive lessons: basic rhythm theory; major and minor blues; 8th, 16th and triplets; extensions; passing chords; lead-rhythm style; funky blues; jump blues; blues rock; and more.
00696038 Book/Online Audio $22.99

HAL•LEONARD®

Order these and more publications from your favorite music retailer at halleonard.com

Prices, availability, and contents subject to change without notice.